Skate Girls

By Patty Segovia

The Child's World®
www.childsworld.com

Published in the United States of America by The Child's World®
P.O. Box 326 • Chanhassen, MN 55317-0326
800-599-READ • www.childsworld.com

ACKNOWLEDGMENTS

The Child's World®: Mary Berendes, Publishing Director

Produced by Shoreline Publishing Group LLC
President / Editorial Director: James Buckley, Jr.
Designer: Tom Carling, carlingdesign.com
Cover Art: Slimfilms
Copy Editor: Beth Adelman

Photo Credits:
Cover—Patty Segovia (3)
Interior—All photographs by Patty Segovia except the following:
Corbis: 5, 11; Getty Images: 6, 8, 10, 12 bottom, 24; iStock: 12

LIBRARY OF CONGRESS CATALOGING-IN-PUBLICATION DATA

Segovia, Patty.
  Skate girls / by Patty Segovia.
     p. cm. — (Girls rock!)
  Includes bibliographical references and index.
  ISBN 1-59296-748-5 (library bound : alk. paper)
 1. Skateboarders—United States—Biography—Juvenile
literature. 2. Sports for women—United States—Juvenile
literature. I. Title. II. Series.
  GV859.812.S44 2006
  796.22092'2—dc22
                           2006009024

CONTENTS

SKATEBOARDING Rocks!

Skateboarding is a cool and fun sport. Girls all over the world are skateboarding. It's so popular that companies now design skateboards, clothing, and shoes just for girls.

Skateboarding champ Cara Beth Burnside says, "The future of skateboarding is the younger girls coming up. They have a lot of older girls to look up to now. You can see girls skating in magazines and on TV. The more girls see that, the more it is going to inspire them!"

So let's get inspired!

One of the coolest things about skateboarding is having fun with your friends.

Did you ever wonder how skateboarding got started? In the 1950s, the first skateboards were just pieces of wood with roller-skate wheels attached. The wheels were made of clay and metal and didn't grip the road well at all. This led to accidents. In fact, early skateboards were kind of dangerous!

In 1973, inventor Frank Nasworthy created a new kind of plastic wheel. These new wheels gave skaters more control and a better grip on the road. The wheels led to a skateboard boom. By the late 1970s, skateboard magazines and skate parks were appearing everywhere.

Here's a 1960s skateboarder doing a simple kick-turn on a wooden board with clay wheels.

Cool move! National champion Pat McGee posed for this 1965 Life *magazine cover to show that girls could ride skateboards, too.*

The craze and
the menace of
SKATEBOARDS

San Diego's Pat McGee,
national girls' champion,
does a handstand on wheels

MAY 14 · 1965 · 35¢

Only a few girls used skateboards in those early days. Girls who had done gymnastics were often very good skaters.

Some women skaters became well known. Millions of people saw Pat McGee's photo on the cover of *Life*. Laura Thornhill won several big events and became well known, too. She was one of the first girls to have a skateboard sold with her name on it.

Other Tricky Girls

Ellen O'Neal was known for a trick called "daffy," in which a skater does **wheelies** on two boards at the same time. Ellen Berryman was known for combining her gymnastics skills with skating. Robin Logan was the first girl to do a **kick flip**. Kim Cespedes was a star in the 1970s and still competes in downhill and **slalom** events today.

In the 1970s, skate parks opened up a whole new world of skateboarding tricks. The parks had ramps and slopes instead of just flat surfaces like the streets. Awesome new tricks were created in a new style called "vert," which is short for **vertical**.

This daring skater zooms up a skate-park wall.

In vert skateboarding, riders make use of walls, ramps, and slopes, often shooting down one side and flying up the other. Sometimes they fly high in the air and do cool tricks before they land— safely, they hope!

Top female vert skaters in those days included Patty Hoffman, Vicki Vickers, and Teri Lawrence. They all **ripped** hard! Peggy Oki was also a star street skater. She still skates today.

Like many skateboarding words, "rip" comes from surfing. It means to perform tricks.

Skateboarding hit hard times in the 1980s. Many skate parks closed because riders weren't coming. Both **BMX cycling** and in-line skating drew kids away from the sport. Many skate parks closed because riders weren't coming.

Loyal skaters stuck with it, though, and kept the sport alive. And girl skaters were among them! In 1989, the Women's Skateboard Network was created to help girls find out about the sport and to find places to skate.

In the past 10 years, skateboarding has caught on again. The X Games (see page 24) have turned skaters into superstars. Girls are a big part of this skateboarding scene. Let's meet some of today's top skaters.

The Summer X Games began in 1995. They are held every year in a different city. The Games include skateboarding, stunt bike riding, and other action sports.

BEST IN THE World

The skateboarding boom has turned some girl skaters into stars. They're successful because of their hard work and amazing skills.

Skateboard star Cara Beth Burnside was also an awesome **snowboarder**. In fact, she finished fourth at the 1998 Winter Olympics. Cara Beth used the same sort of skills to become a top skateboarder, too. She won a gold medal at the 2005 X Games and won the 2004 All Girl Skate Jam, too. Way to go!

Elissa rides a rail during a street competition. In this event, skaters do tricks on rails, stairs, and ramps that look like a real street scene.

Elissa Steamer has been a big star for several years. She has won several X Games events and won a gold medal at the Gravity Games, too. In 2004, she became the first (and so far the only) girl to star in a popular video game based on superstar skateboarder Tony Hawk.

Skateboarders often live colorful lives. Heidi Fitzgerald is colorful in person, too! She's as well known for her tattoos as for her great skating. Heidi has skated in all the top events, and especially loves street skating. She uses her creative ideas to invent new tricks.

Heidi puts on a great show—on her board or just showing her tattoos!

Here Lyn-Z shows off a "grab," reaching down to hold onto the board with her hand.

One of the youngest and most talented skaters is Lyn-Z Adams Hawkins. Known by her nickname of "Punky Brewster" (from a 1980s TV show), Lyn-Z fears no trick. In 2003, she won the All Girl Skate Jam vert event when she was just 13. She was the vert champion at the 2004 X Games. In 2005, when she was only 15, she landed a 60-foot (18-m) ramp jump!

When Apryl Woodcock was a kid, she turned to skateboarding to help her through some rough times. It didn't take her long to get very, very good! Apryl turned pro at 12 years old, inspired by superstar Tony Hawk. Apryl stays busy when she's not skating, too. She visits schools to give kids positive messages —stay in school, and stay away from drugs.

Apryl does a "grind" move, riding along the edge of the vert ramp.

Vanessa Torres, who's from California, didn't start skating until she was 19—much later than most skaters. She made up for lost time quickly and became a winner—including winning X Games gold medals in street skating.

Vanessa also cares deeply about the environment. When a skateboard company signed her up to use their products, she made sure that her skateboards were made without cutting down too many trees.

On the long list of future skateboarding stars, look for Rebecca Syracopoulos. Becky has finished near the top of several important events and hopes to break through to the top of the sport soon.

Vanessa gets big air when launching off this graffiti-covered bump.

Most swimming pools have straight sides that make skating a challenge. Skate parks have rounded pools for better skating.

Kim Peterson says her gymnastics background is one reason she's a top skater. Her great body control has helped her become a great **pool skater**. She has finished in the top three of events held in empty, curved swimming pools, such as the one shown on the right.

Not Just Girls

Guys are great skateboarders, too! Tony Hawk has won more X-Games medals than any other skater. Danny Way (left) is awesome in the air. In 2005, he used a ramp to jump over the Great Wall of China.

Mimi Knoop not only has great skateboarding skills, she has a great attitude. Like most top skaters, she doesn't think winning is the most important thing about her sport. She says, "Just have fun, do what you want to do, and don't worry about anything else. Skateboarding is about having a good time."

Skate star Mimi Knoop is ready to swoop down the side of this empty pool.

SKATE GIRLS in Action!

Today, fans of skateboarding can see their heroes in many big events. One of the biggest is the Summer X Games, first called the Extreme Games when they began in 1995. Held in a different city each year, the X Games give lots of people a chance to see skateboarding and other action sports. And if you can't go in person, the X Games are shown on national TV.

The X Games feature two types of skateboarding: street and vert. Street skaters go through a cement course with ramps, jumps, and **obstacles**. Vert skaters ride up the sides of a U-shaped wall called a half-pipe.

Girls love to skate! Here's a group photo of the skaters from the 2005 All Girl Skate Jam.

The All Girl Skate Jam (AGSJ) was founded in 1990 as a way to recognize and celebrate women who loved to ride skateboards.

There are lots of skating events for boys. But the AGSJ was the first skateboarding competition for girls of all ages and

abilities. Fans can watch the main event in San Diego, California. Girls who want to learn to skate can attend AGSJ camps in different cities.

There are plenty of top skaters from other countries, too! Two of the international superstars to watch are 2005 AGSJ champ Alison "Nugget" Matasi from Canada and 14-year-old Karen Feliosa from Brazil. Nugget has done well at AGSJ events, and Karen is the top girl skater in her whole country! Evelien Bouillart of Belgium is only 15, but she has already been in the X Games.

Skateboarding is a really great way to spend time with

AGSJ tours nationally and internationally, uniting professional and amateur girls from around the world to skate competitively and have fun.

your friends, get some exercise, or just show off your skills! So strap on your helmet, get out your knee pads, and try one of the hottest sports for girls today.

"Nugget"
Matasi holds a skateboard doll as she rides on this mini-ramp.

GLOSSARY

BMX cycling a type of bicycle riding done with smaller bikes on hilly dirt tracks

kick flip a skateboard trick in which the rider jumps off the ground with the board and flips the board around before landing back on it

obstacles objects on which skaters can perform tricks

pool skater a person who skates in empty, slope-sided home swimming pools

rip skateboarding term for performing tricks very well

slalom an event where racers take turns zigzagging between gates

snowboarder a person who rides a snowboard, which is like a surfboard used on snow

street a type of skateboarding done over objects made to look like a real street scene

vertical in skateboarding, a type of skating done up and down the sides of a U-shaped ramp

wheelies a skateboard trick in which the skater pops the back or front wheels off the ground while keeping the other two wheels on the ground

FIND OUT MORE

BOOKS

The Concrete Wave: The History of Skateboarding
by Michael Brooke
(Warwick Publishing, Toronto) 2003
From the sport's early days to today's X-Games superstars, this photo-filled book covers all the key moments in skateboarding.

No Limits: Skateboarding
by Jed Morgan
(Franklin Watts, Danbury, CT) 2005
Read an overview of skateboarding, including names of tricks and photos of stars, in this book.

Skateboarding Is Not a Crime: 50 Years of Street Culture
by James Davis
(Firefly Books, Inc., New York) 2004
This book focuses on the style and fashion of skateboarding more than the sport itself.

Skater Girl: A Girl's Guide to Skateboarding
by Patty Segovia and Rebecca Heller
(Ulysses Press, Berkeley, CA) 2006
Cowritten by the author of the book you're reading now, it includes step-by-step guides to important tricks.

WEB SITES

Visit our home page for lots of links about skateboarding:
www.childsworld.com/links

Note to Parents, Teachers, and Librarians: We routinely check our Web links to make sure they're safe, active sites—so encourage your readers to check them out!

INDEX

PATTY SEGOVIA is a photographer, producer, agent, and author, whose most recent work is *Skater Girl: A Girl's Guide to Skateboarding*. She founded and continues to organize the All Girl Skate Jam. Segovia and AGSJ have been featured in many national magazines, including *Latina*, and her photographs have appeared in *Sports Illustrated for Women* and *Time Magazine*. She also hosts an Internet radio show about the AGSJ.